YOUR KNOWLEDGE HAS VALUE

Bibliographic information published by the German National Library:

The German National Library lists this publication in the National Bibliography;
detailed bibliographic data are available on the Internet at http://dnb.dnb.de .

Imprint:

Copyright © 2015 GRIN Verlag, Open Publishing GmbH
Print and binding: Books on Demand GmbH, Norderstedt Germany
ISBN: 9783668417298

Luqman Adedokun

The Implication of the West African Power Pool (WAPP) to the Electricity Supply Industry (ESI) in Nigeria

GRIN Publishing

GRIN - Your knowledge has value

Since its foundation in 1998, GRIN has specialized in publishing academic texts by students, college teachers and other academics as e-book and printed book. The website www.grin.com is an ideal platform for presenting term papers, final papers, scientific essays, dissertations and specialist books.

Visit us on the internet:

http://www.grin.com/

http://www.facebook.com/grincom

http://www.twitter.com/grin_com

THE IMPLICATION OF THE WEST AFRICAN POWER POOL (WAPP) TO THE ELECTRITY SUPPLY INDUSTRY (ESI) IN NIGERIA.

BY: ADEDOKUN LUQMAN ADEBAYO[1]

---

[1] PhD Student in the field of Environmental Law and Sustainable Development at the Atlantic International University, Honolulu, Hawai, United States.

TABLE OF CONTENTS

Abstract

This paper discusses the history, vision and mission of the West African Power Pool, as well as its successes and constraints then appraising its impact on the Nigeria electricity supply industry using the doctrinal research methodology.

Keywords

West African Power Pool, Power, Nigeria electricity industry, power generation.

1.   INTRODUCTION

In December 1999 the Heads of State and Government of member states of the Economic Community of West Africa States (ECOWAS) created the West African Power Pool (WAPP) with 14 out of 15 member states agreeing to pool together the efforts of their various national electricity utilities. The goal is to create more robust regional power systems that will reduce capital investments expenditure, lower systems operational costs and increase electricity supply and access in the region.[2] Fifteen years down the line, WAPP has had limited impact on the electricity supply of the region, making the region's aspiration to realize energy security a myth of some sort as over half of the population in the region lacks access to electricity.[3]

Nigeria a member of ECOWAS and a participating country in the WAPP project is expected to contribute immensely to this regional power pool being the region's primary supplier of natural gas, and also accounting for about 43.4% of regional hydropower generation,[4] yet the country is bedevilled with serious electricity supply problems. Some of which include: high level of transmission and distribution losses. In fact the poor electricity supply in Nigeria makes the country the largest importer of generator in the world as a large number of its citizenry use generators as substitute for failed public electricity supply.[5] This paper shall thus attempt to discuss the paradox of Nigeria's electricity supply dearth and its role in the realization of the WAPP.

2.   HISTORY, VISION AND MISSION OF WEST AFRICAN POWER POOL

The West African power pool (WAPP) is a specialized institution of the Economic Community of the West African States (ECOWAS) consisting of fourteen countries namely: Benin, Burkina Faso, Cote D'Ivoire, Ghana, Niger, Nigeria, Togo, Guinea, Guinea Bissau,

---

[2] Manji Cheto, Kathryn Brooks (2013) Africa In-Depth West Africa: Pooling together for Power retrieved from africapractice.com accessed last on 19/09/2015
[3] Ibid
[4] Ibid
[5] Akin Iwayemi, ed. Energy Resources and Development in Nigeria retrieved from www.naee.org.ng/files/EnergyResourcesandDevelopmentinNigeria.pdf accessed last on 29/09/2016

Liberia, Mali, Senegal, Sierra Leone, The Gambia generating about 10, 000MW for an average population of about 340 million people within the region.[6]

The vision of WAPP is to integrate the national power systems of participating states into a unified regional electricity market – with the expectation that such mechanism would over the medium to long term, ensure the citizens of ECOWAS member states with a stable and reliable electricity supply at competitive costs.[7]

WAPP's mission is to promote and develop infrastructure for power generation and transmission, and assure the coordination of electric power exchanges between ECOWAS member states.[8]

With respect to its organizational structure, WAPP has an executive board, organizational committees, a general secretariat, information and coordination centre, administration and finance department, planning investment programming and environmental safeguards department all responsible to the General Assembly created in July 2006 by a joint agreement of National utilities in West Africa.[9]

3.   ASSESSMENT OF THE WEST AFRICAN POWER POOL

The West African region produces about 40,000GWh of electricity with thermal plants contributing about 64%, hydro 31%, imported energy sources 5%.[10] Prior to the formation of WAPP cross-border trading of electricity took place between certain countries in the region,[11] however, WAPP's existence has increased cross-border electricity flow and merged interconnections. For example, gas supply under the West Africa Gas Pipelines supports power production in Ghana.[12]

---

[6] Babtunde Adeyemo (2014) West African Power Pool [a paper presented at South Asia Regional Workshop on Competitive Electricity Markets, held at Colombo Sri Lanka]
WAPP took a clue from the South African Power Pool developed by a team of researchers from Purdue University, USA on this see Dike, D.O and Obah, O.B 'Restructuring of the West African Power Pool (WAPP) Transmission System Purdue Model
[7] Ibid
[8] Ibid
[9] Ibid
[10] Ibid
[11] For example between 1979 – 1989 Nigeria and Ghana traded excess capacity, while Nigeria also supplied Niger with electricity
[12] Beks Dagogo-Jack (2012) Status of Nigeria Power Reform [a paper presented at the Annual West African Power Industry Convention (WAPIC) 2012] for the Presidential Task Force on Power retrieved from www.nigeriapowerreform.org accessed last on 29/09/2015

WAPP's Master Plan first adopted in 1999 was revised in 2005 and 2012 is being implemented as WAPP's priority projects – requiring the utilization of diverse energy source in the region for power generation; construction of transmission lines to interconnect countries within the region.[13] It is noteworthy that countries within the region have rich endowments of fossil fuels with great renewable energy potentials[14], although a number of the countries import fuel for power generation.

Out of WAPP's twenty-four priority projects, four have been commissioned and are operational[15], the remaining are either at implementation stages or pre-investment stage though quite a number of them have failed to meet their commissioning date. To provide energy for the poor, WAPP came up with medium voltage cross-border electrification sub-program with twelve projects. It has successfully commissioned two, six of the projects are under development and the rest at implementation stages.[16]

The Legal framework upon which WAPP operates is the ECOWAS Treaty, the Energy Act or ECOWAS Energy Protocol which establishes the legal framework for securing competitive market. WAPP's prospects includes: the West Africa Gas Pipeline project, large regional electricity market.

WAPP's constraints includes: inadequate generation [most of the generating plants in participating countries are aged/old and majorly constructed during colonial period or shortly after independence and are unable to meet current demand]; undiversified energy mix; weak national transmission network; supply problems to three land locked countries; limited interconnection for cross-border electricity trade and lack of funding.[17] The issue of lack of

---

[13] Babatunde Adeyemo (2014) *op cit*
[14] Nigeria and Ghana have huge oil and gas resources [recently Cote D'Ivoire discovered oil reserves in its coastline borders with Ghana]; Senegal, Niger and Nigeria have huge coal reserves. Guinea has huge water resources; and all the countries in the region have great potentials for solar and biomass power generation.
[15] The operational projects include: 330KV Aboadze (Ghana) – Volta (Ghana) commissioned in 2010; the 330KV Sakete (Benin) – Ikeja West (Nigeria) commissioned in 2007; the 225KV Bobo Dioulasso (Burkina Faso) – Ouagadougou (Burkina Faso) commissioned in 2009; the Ferkessedougou (Cote D'Ivoire) – Sikasso (Mali) – Segou (Mali) commissioned in 2012. On this, see Babatunde Adeyemo (2014) *op cit*
[16] Babatunde Adeyemo (2014) *op cit* under the medium voltage cross-border electrification sub-program there has been electrification of 12 rural communities in Togo from Ghana; 7 rural communities in Burkina Faso also from Ghana
[17] Ibid

funding is unarguably a major constraint as WAPP's projects are capital intensive and far exceed the financial capacities of participating member states.[18]

4.   AN OVERVIEW OF THE NIGERIAN ELECTRICITY INDUSTRY

Though electricity generation in Nigeria began in 1896,[19] more than a century ago, it can only boast of 40Kw/thousand inhabitants[20]with an installed generation capacity of 10, 000MW with peak generation of 4, 500MW.[21] Only about 40% of the Nigerian population have access to electricity, the poor electricity supply in Nigeria despite its rich endowments in energy sources has created the world's highest concentration of small-scale power supply, with many Nigerians making use of generators to produce required electricity.[22]

Prior to the power sector reform, the National Electric Power Authority (NEPA) a vertically integrated government monopoly supervised by the Federal Ministry of Power managed the Nigeria electricity industry. As part of the reforms, NEPA metamorphosed to Power Holding Company of Nigeria (PHCN) which following the enactment of the Electric Power Sector Reform Act (EPSRA) 2005 was unbundled into the Transmission Company of Nigeria, 6 generating companies (GenCos) and 11 distribution companies (DisCos) - thus making the Nigeria electricity industry one of the most liberalised in Africa.[23]

The Nigerian Electricity Regulatory Commission (NERC) and the Rural Electrification Agency (REA)[24] were established by the EPSRA, 2005 to oversee, coordinate and regulate the Nigeria electricity industry, the latter body restricted to rural electrification responsible to the Minister of Power.[25] Other relevant authorities in the Nigeria electricity industry includes: Nigerian Bulk Electricity Trading Company Plc (NBET), Nigeria Electricity Liability

---

[18] Retrieved from ecowapp.org accessed last on 27/03/2016
[19] Ayodele Oni (2013) "The Nigerian Electric Power Sector – Policy, Law, Negotiation strategy, Business" printed by CI – Plus Nigeria at page 2
[20] Beks Dagogo-Jack (2012) *op cit*
[21] Investment Opportunities in the Nigerian Power Sector retrieved from www.nigeriapowerreform.org accessed last on 29/09/2015. Klut Findt, De Buy Scott and Dr Christain Lindfield (2014) Sub-Saharan Africa Power Outlook obtained from kpmg.co.za last visited 29/09/2015 submit that Nigeria's installed capacity is 11, 542.2MW as at 2014 and access to electricity was 50% of the population
[22] Klut Findt, De Buy Scott and Dr Christain Lindfield (2014) *op cit*
[23] Ibid
[24] See Sections 32 and 88 of the Electric Power Sector Reform Act, 2005
[25] Basically the Federal Ministry of Power and NERC maintain oversight functions over the power sector, while bodies like the Presidential Task Force on Power, Bureau for Public Enterprises, and Presidential Action Committee on Power played contributory roles in the power sector reform.

Management Company, Nigeria Atomic Energy Commission, Energy Commission of Nigeria.

The laws regulating the sector include the EPSRA, 2005, the Constitution of the Federal Republic of Nigeria, 1999 (as amended) and state laws like Ekiti State Electricity Board Law 2012[26].

The Nigerian electricity industry is powered mainly by thermal and hydro power-plants but the country is endowed with other natural resources that can improve its energy mix to include: coal, solar, wind, nuclear, modernised biomass. Issues like pipeline vandalism, theft of transmission cables are recurrent problems hampering the effectiveness and efficiency of the Nigeria electricity industry. Another problem in the Nigeria electricity supply industry is the neglect and/or refusal of public authorities to pay up their electricity bills.[27]

5. AN APPRAISAL OF THE WEST AFRICAN POWER POOL'S IMPACT ON THE NIGERIAN ELECTRICITY SUPPLY INDUSTRY

As have been earlier stated the WAPP aims at integrating the national power systems of member states into an unified regional electricity market, this vision has medium and long term implications on the Nigerian electricity supply industry especially with its ongoing reforms.

Under the WAPP, Nigeria has a power sale obligation of 150MW with a request for upward review to 200MW in the short term for the Transmission Company of Benin and Togo known as CEB – (Community Electric du Benin).[28] This power sale obligation was further reviewed upwards recently from 200MW to 300MW.[29] Nigeria also has gas supply obligations under the West African Gas Pipelines projects that serves as a feeder into the West African Power

---

[26] This law establishes the Electricity Board of Ekiti state as a body corporate with powers and responsibilities with includes: the power to establish state electric power stations. On this see Section 5 of the Ekiti state Electricity Board (Establishment) Law, 2012

[27] The unpleasant altercation that occurs when agents of DisCos approach these public authorities is far to be desired for the effectiveness of the power sector. Reports of Military men beating up distributing companies staff who approach the authority for payment of their electricity bills or attempt to disconnect them for failing to pay their bills regrettably abound.

[28] Bek Dagogo-Jack (2012) *op cit*

[29] Retrieved from www.medianigeria.com last accessed 06/10/2015 Under the upward review 200MW of power supply goes to the Community Electric du Benin – the Transmission Company for Benin and Togo and the balance of 100MW is given to Niger Republic

Pool and passes through Benin and Togo and for which it pays penalties when it fails to meet its obligations under the project. Constant gas pipelines vandalism have made power supply within the country erratic,[30] yet Nigeria desires to develop additional thermal generation plants to increase its domestic generation, and this will result in an overall increase in West Africa's regional power generation.

Ironically, the increase of thermal generation plants in Nigeria constructed by private entities could undermine WAPP's plans as the political importance of the Nigeria's privatisation means that the government will be likely hesitant in the short to medium term to commit to exporting power or gas to the rest of the region at a time when the country needs it most.[31]

Nigeria's population is rapidly increasing and its economy is likewise growing which means that the demand for electricity is also on the increase, and where the current electricity supply barely meets the citizenry, manufacturing industries it would be impulsive to insist on exporting power to other countries within the West Africa region to meet obligations under WAPP. This notwithstanding, it should be noted that prior to the existence of WAPP, Nigeria exports power to Niger Republic and part of Benin, between 1979 – 1989 it also trade excess power capacity to Ghana.[32]

Considering Nigeria's power sale obligation arising from the pool, one may be forced to ask what is the logic behind WAPP, if Nigeria is to supply 200MW of electricity to Benin and Togo and 100MW to Niger Republic when it can as well divest the said power to meet its electricity need?

The answer to this may have more socio-economic leaning, as providing electricity to these countries could aid them in addressing social, economic and political problems which if not addressed could possibly lead to disorder within these countries. Then Nigeria would still have a responsibility to help check the crisis since these countries share borders with Nigeria. In other words, Nigeria's action in supplying electricity to these countries while its citizens electricity demand and need are still yet to be met could help check mass migration of

---

[30] See Clement Adeyinka Oke (2015) Nigeria Power Sector Reform: Status, Progress and Outlook [a paper presented at the 2015 Academy Technology Dinner Lecture held at Lagos, Nigeria for the Presidential Task Force on Power] retrieved from www.nigeriapowerreform.org accessed last on 22/12/2015
[31] Manji Cheto and Kathryn Brooks (2013) *op cit*
[32] Babatunde Adeyemo (2014) *op cit*

citizens of these energy importing states to Nigeria. Besides, these countries pay for the electricity supplied to them.

Another implication of WAPP on the Nigerian electricity supply industry would be as it pertains to the existing legal and regulatory framework of the electricity industry in Nigeria. If WAPP is to operate optimally, integrated transmission utilities, special purpose companies will have to be formed, these utilities or companies may end up either creating a competitive market in the region or result in having frictions with existing national power companies and utilities especially if the regional utilities are not liberalised.

Arguing from the viewpoint of the increasing collapse of nation-states for supranational bodies, it is submitted that WAPP if efficiently implemented will aid the speedy development of additional power generation plants in Nigeria, and more transmission lines. Some of the land locked countries within the region share borders with Nigeria as such transmission lines will have to be constructed in Nigeria for such countries to partake of the power pool. For example, WAPP's project in Nigeria includes: the 330KV WAPP North Core Transmission Project in Birnin Kebbi, Nigeria, which is replicated in: Niamey (Niger Republic), Ougadougou (Burkina Faso), and Bemebreke (Benin Republic); 2nd Line 330KV Ikeja West Transmission Line which is replicated in Sakete (Benin Republic).

The privatisation exercise of the remaining government-owned power plants under the National Integrated Power Project which provides electricity to Benin and Togo (inclusive of Niger Republic) will require the power utilities of these countries to sign a power purchase agreement with the Nigeria Electricity Bulk Trader Plc and be up to date in their payments for electricity.[33]

Unlike some ECOWAS countries that import electricity to meet their energy demand, the Nigerian electricity supply industry is not dependent on the West African Power Pool, the existence of the pool would one way or the other succeed in contributing to the increase of power generation, transmission and distribution in Nigeria although under the pool Nigeria will still have to supply electricity while its energy need have not be fully met. The resultant

---

[33] These were the comments of Dr Sam Amadi to the CEB team when the team raised the issue of the implication of the privatisation of the NIPP that supplies them electricity retrieved from www.medianigeria.com last accessed on 06/10/2015

increase in power generation triggered by WAPP in Nigeria will also assist in meeting its energy needs.

6. CONCLUSION AND RECOMMENDATION

Nigeria is a member of the Executive Board of WAPP and owing to its "big brother" disposition, it is not likely to renege on its obligation to the pool notwithstanding the current state of its electricity supply industry. With the ongoing reforms in the Nigeria power sector, its increasing population and demand for electricity, increase in domestic power generation will ultimately result in an overall increase in West Africa's regional power generation.

The Nigeria electricity supply industry is undergoing reforms and Nigeria is not likely going to jeopardise its interests to meet its obligations under WAPP. This seems to be the position of the Chairman of NERC, Dr Sam Amadi who while speaking to the delegation from the Transmission Company of Benin and Togo – CEB when the company recently requested for an upward review of the amount of power supplied to it by Nigeria under its power sale obligation stated "the ongoing reform in the Nigeria electricity industry will not jeopardise international relations and strategic interests of Nigeria".[34]

RECOMMENDATIONS

To successfully realize its vision and mission, it is recommended that WAPP and the Nigeria electricity supply industry:

- ❖ Diversify its energy mix.
- ❖ Construct stand-alone grids to provide electricity to rural communities.
- ❖ In diversifying its energy mix and creating stand-alone grids explore the options of renewable energy.

---

[34] Retrieved from www.medianigeria.com

REFERENCES

1. Ayodele Oni (2013) "The Nigerian Electric Power Sector – Policy, Law, Negotiation strategy, Business" printed by CI – Plus Nigeria at page 2.

2. Akin Iwayemi, ed. Energy Resources and Development in Nigeria retrieved from www.naee.org.ng/files/EnergyResourcesandDevelopmentinNigeria.pdf accessed last on 29/09/2015.

3. Babtunde Adeyemo (2014) West African Power Pool [a paper presented at South Asia Regional Workshop on Competitive Electricity Markets, held at Colombo Sri Lanka].

4. Beks Dagogo-Jack (2012) Status of Nigeria Power Reform [a paper presented at the Annual West African Power Industry Convention (WAPIC) 2012] for the Presidential Task Force on Power retrieved from www.nigeriapowerreform.org

5. Clement Adeyinka Oke (2015) Nigeria Power Sector Reform: Status, Progress and Outlook [a paper presented at the 2015 Academy Technology Dinner Lecture held at Lagos, Nigeria for the Presidential Task Force on Power] retrieved from www.nigeriapowerreform.org

6. Klut Findt, De Buy Scott and Dr Christain Lindfield (2014) Sub-Saharan Africa Power Outlook obtained from kpmg.co.za

7. Investment Opportunities in the Nigerian Power Sector retrieved from www.nigeriapowerreform.org

8. Manji Cheto, Kathryn Brooks (2013) Africa In-Depth West Africa: Pooling together for Power retrieved from africapractice.com

9. www.ecowapp.org

10. www.medianigeria.com